Natural Words

A Dictionary For Naturalists

Kelby & Amy Ouchley

Copyright © 2019 Kelby & Amy Ouchley

First Edition

All rights reserved. No part of this book may be reproduced or transmitted in any form by any means, electronic or mechanical, including photocopying and recording, or by any information or storage retrieval system, except as may be expressly permitted by the 1976 Copyright Act or by the authors. Requests for permission should be made in writing through the authors' contact page at http://bayou-diversity.com

ISBN: 978-1691274970

This book may be available in e-book format from Amazon and other fine e-book vendors.

DEDICATION

We dedicate this book to our family in hopes that the written word will bring them as much joy as it has us.

FOREWORD

As biologists and environmental educators, we recognize the terminology of our trade is often foreign to those who seek to learn more about the natural world. In compiling this small book we hope to address that issue. We would like to think that *Natural Words* is a dictionary for naturalists (**naturalist** – student of natural history, as a hobby or professionally). By definition, **natural history** is the study of living organisms and their non-living environment, usually by observation. The book contains those unique words that one might hear in a ranger's campfire talk, or read in a conservation magazine or scientific article. They express the physical description, behavior, classification, and life history of living organisms. They depict those words that illustrate the environment in which the organisms are found. Simply put, this small dictionary is geared toward all nature lovers with an interest in learning the terminology used to relate to the natural world.

Many sources were consulted to craft definitions that best fit the purpose of this book. Some words have multiple meanings. In these cases, only those definitions relevant to natural history are used. Definitions often include words that are defined elsewhere in the text. When this occurs these words are italicized at their first mention in a definition to provide additional context. Examples are also included in many cases to aid understanding. Of course, many more relevant words could be added to this dictionary (and perhaps will be in future editions), but we hope that those included here will provide a foundation of *Natural Words*.

NATURAL WORDS

NATURAL WORDS

A

abiotic – non-living components of the *environment*, usually chemical or physical parts such as minerals, moisture, temperature and sunlight.

achene – a dry fruit containing one seed formed from a single *carpal*. The fruits of many plants are achenes, including some in the rose and sedge families.

adaptation – any trait of an *organism* that helps it survive and successfully reproduce in its *environment*. Thick bark is an adaptation of some *tree*s that enables them to live in fire prone areas.

aerie – nest of a large *bird* of prey, especially an eagle, often in a high, inaccessible place.

aerobic – requiring or living in the presence of oxygen. Most but not all *organisms* need oxygen for *respiration*. See *anaerobic*.

albinism – in animals, a hereditary condition that results in a lack of pigment in the skin, hair or feathers. Albinos appear white with pink eyes.

alevin – a newly hatched *fish* still carrying the yolk sac, used in reference to trout and salmon.

NATURAL WORDS

algae – large group of plant-like mostly *aquatic organism*s that are distinguished from others by having simple, single-celled reproductive organs. Most algae have *chlorophyll* but lack true leaves, stems and roots. Diatoms, kelp and sargassum are types of algae.

algal bloom – rapid, often unnatural growth of *algae* in freshwater or the sea that can produce toxic effects on humans and aquatic life such as *fish*, shellfish, marine *mammal*s and *bird*s. Algae blooms often occur when heavy loads of nutrients from sewage or agricultural fertilizers enter a water body.

alluvial soil – sediments deposited by flowing water, as that occurring with overbank flooding and in river deltas. See *loess*.

altricial – in *mammal*s and *bird*s, those hatched or born in a helpless, undeveloped state requiring attentive parental care to survive. Cottontail rabbits and songbirds are altricial.

amphibian – group of *ectothermic*, *vertebrate* animals that includes frogs, toads, salamanders, and caecilians. Most *species* have an early *aquatic* stage before they undergo *metamorphosis* and become air-breathing adults.

anadromous – characteristic of *fish* that migrate from salt water *habitat* into freshwater in order to *spawn*. American shad and most salmon are examples of anadromous fish. See *catadromous*.

anaerobic – not requiring or living in the presence of oxygen. Some types of *bacteria* are anaerobic. See *aerobic*.

annual – in plants, those *species* that complete their *life cycle* including germination, reproduction, and death in one year. Bluebonnet and coreopsis are examples of annual wildflowers. See *biennial* and *perennial*.

anthropogenic – describes something made or caused by humans, such as *pollution* or changes to natural landscapes.

NATURAL WORDS

anthropomorphism – giving human traits to nonhumans, especially animals. *Winnie-the-Pooh*, and *Animal Farm* are examples of books with anthropomorphic characters.

apex predator – those *predator*s at the top of a *food chain* that have no natural predators themselves. Alligators, great horned owls, and orcas are apex predators.

aquatic – living or growing in water.

aquifer – underground formation of porous, water-bearing rock.

arachnid – group of *arthropods* that includes spiders, mites, scorpions, ticks, harvestmen, and wind scorpions. Common characteristics include eight legs and no antennae.

arboreal – living in *tree*s, usually in reference to animals. Flying squirrels and tree frogs are arboreal.

arboretum – botanical collection of living *tree*s used for education, research, and/or enjoyment.

arthropod – broad group of *invertebrate*s that includes *insect*s, spiders, *crustacean*s, and others. Common characteristics are an external skeleton, jointed legs in pairs, and a segmented body. More than 80 percent of all known *species* on earth are arthropods.

asexual reproduction – in some plants and simple animals, reproduction by one individual without the joining of sex cells from two different parents. See *sexual reproduction*.

axil – in *botany*, the place where a leaf joins the stem.

NATURAL WORDS

B

bacteria – large group of microscopic *organism*s that can be free-living or parasitic; usually single-celled. All forms of life are dependent on bacteria as *decomposer*s in *soil* that make food available to plants. Many animals including humans require gut bacteria for digestion. They are a source of antibiotics but also cause diseases such as tuberculosis, diphtheria, typhoid, and pneumonia.

ballooning – type of flying behavior used by spiders and some other *arthropod*s in which they emit and ride drifting strands of silk for vast distances, presumably as a means of dispersal beneficial to the *species*. Natural electric fields in the atmosphere have been shown to aid the process.

bask – in animals, to expose a part of the body to the sun's rays in order to absorb heat energy. Many types of animals bask including some butterflies, snakes, turtles, *bird*s, and *mammal*s.

NATURAL WORDS

bayou – small, natural waterway that flows through swamps and other lowlands, especially in Louisiana.

benthos – *organism*s that live on or in the bottom of oceans, lakes or other water bodies. Oysters, flounders, and rooted seagrasses are benthic organisms.

berry – in *botany*, a thick, fleshy fruit with many small seeds developed from a single ovary. Technically, grapes and elderberries produce berries. Strawberries and blackberries do not.

biennial – in plants, those species that complete their *life cycle* in two years, growing in the first, then reproducing and dying in the second. Black-eyed Susan and Queen Anne's lace are examples of biennial wildflowers. See *annual* and *perennial*.

big game – large *species* of animals that are hunted for food and/or sport. Big game animals are usually mammals like deer or elk, or *fish* such as marlin. See *small game*.

bilateral symmetry – in *biology*, body plan of some *organism*s that have mirror image sides when divided down the midline. Most animals, including humans, have bilateral symmetry. See *radial symmetry*.

binomial nomenclature – in *biology*, the practice of using two names (*genus* and *species*) to denote every species of *organism*; also called the scientific name, e.g. *Homo sapiens* (human), *Quercus alba* (white oak), *Danaus plexippus* (monarch butterfly).

bioaccumulation – process by which some toxic substances such as *pesticide*s and heavy metals, become concentrated in the body. The bioaccumulation of DDT in bald eagles threatened the *species* with *extirpation* in the lower 48 states at one time.

biocentrism – in ethics, a viewpoint that deems inherent value in all non-human life.

biodegradable – capable of being decomposed by microorganisms such as *bacteria* and *fungi*.

NATURAL WORDS

biodiversity – all the varieties of life forms in a certain area. The area can be as large as planet Earth, where an estimated 10 million *species* of plants, animals, and microbes live (95 percent of which are made up of *arthropod*s and microbes), or as small as an individual gene. It is commonly considered at the scale of *ecosystem*s.

biology – the study of living *organism*s including a host of specialized fields within this broad category.

bioluminescence – the production of light by living *organism*s; caused by a chemical reaction of enzymes and results in very little heat. A wide variety of organisms exhibit bioluminescence including fireflies, glowworms, some *bacteria, fungi, fish*, and beetles.

biomass – in *ecology*, the mass of living *organism*s in a specific area.

biome – large, natural region with characteristic plants and animals. Deserts, coral reefs, *tropical* rain *forest*s, and tallgrass *prairie*s are examples of biomes.

biophilia – human love of other living things and *nature* in general.

biorhythm – recurring cycle of biological processes such as sleep and wake periods, or heart rate fluctuations.

biosphere – parts of the earth and its atmosphere where life can exist.

biota – plant and animal life of a specific region or period of time.

bird – warm-blooded *vertebrate* with wings, feathers, beak, and producing young from eggs; members of the taxonomic *class* Aves. The number of *species* of birds on earth is estimated as high as 18,000.

bog – area of water-saturated soil, often containing peat and characteristic plants such as sphagnum moss.

boreal – in *ecology*, pertaining to those northern areas south of the Arctic, often characterized by *conifer*ous, evergreen *forest*s.

NATURAL WORDS

botany – study of plants.

brackish water – water that contains more salt than fresh water but less than sea water; often found in *estuaries* where fresh water and sea water mix. See *salinity*.

browser – in *ecology*, an *herbivore* that eats leaves, stems, and bark. White-tailed deer and moose are predominantly browsers. See *grazer*.

brumation – in *reptile*s such as snakes and alligators, a condition of torpor when core body temperature decreases and other physiological processes slow down, but not to the extent of that in warm-blooded hibernators (see *hibernation*).

NATURAL WORDS

C

cambium – in woody plants, a layer of tissue between the bark and wood that produces *phloem* cells on the outer side and *xylem* cells on the inner side of the layer; where growth occurs.

canid – member of the dog *family* (Canidae). Foxes, coyotes, wolves, dingoes, jackals, and domestic dogs are canids.

canopy – top layers of *tree* limbs and leaves in a *forest*. Some plants and animals are adapted to live in a forest canopy.

carapace – upper part of a turtle's shell. See *plastron*.

carbon cycle – circulation of carbon atoms throughout all of earth's *ecosystem*s and biotic components by natural processes that include *photosynthesis*, *respiration*, and *decomposition*, and the widespread unnatural process of burning *fossil fuels*.

carnivore – animal that eats meat. Cougars, mink, and wolves are carnivores. See *herbivore*.

NATURAL WORDS

carpal – in flowering plants, the female reproductive organ that contains the ovary.

carrion – decaying flesh of dead animals. Vultures feed on carrion.

carrying capacity – in *ecology*, maximum number of individuals of any *species* that a certain area can support in a healthy, sustainable condition. Availability and quality of food, water, and other *habitat* conditions determine carrying capacity.

catadromous – *fish* that live most of their lives in fresh water but go to the sea to *spawn*. The American eel is catadromous. See *anadromous*.

caudal – in animals, refers to the tail.

cavity tree – *tree*s that contain holes or hollows formed by disease, lightning or other injuries, or excavated by animals. Cavity trees provide critical denning and nesting *habitat* for many *species* of animals but have been greatly reduced in some areas by commercial *forest monoculture*.

chaparral – in *ecology*, a *community* of dense, woody *shrub*s adapted to dry summers and moist winters.

chlorophyll – green pigment found in *algae* and most higher plants; critical component in the process of *photosynthesis* where carbohydrates are manufactured from water and carbon dioxide using energy from the sun.

class – one of the general divisions in the classification of *organism*s; between *phylum* and *order*. Mammalia (*mammal*s) and Reptilia (*reptile*s) are examples of taxonomic classes.

clearcut – forestry practice of removing all *tree*s and *shrub*s from an area, often to promote tree *monoculture* for commercial purposes, or to convert forests to other land types such as row-crop agriculture. Clearcutting contributes to greatly diminished *biodiversity* in some areas.

climate – average *weather* in a region over a long period of time, often determined in thousands or millions of years. See also *weather*, *climate change* and *global warming*.

NATURAL WORDS

climate change – significant long-term changes in weather patterns of a region that can be caused by several factors. See also *climate*, *global warming*, and *weather*.

climax community – in *ecology*, a plant and animal *community* that is relatively stable in *species* composition and in balance with existing environmental conditions; often the end stage of *succession* in a given area. Tall grass *prairie*s and bottomland hardwood *forest*s are examples of climax communities.

commensalism – relationship between two *organism*s in which one benefits and the other neither benefits nor is harmed. Interactions between remora *fish* and sharks, and cattle egrets and cattle are examples of commensalism. See *symbiosis*.

community – in *ecology*, those plants and animals living in a particular *habitat* and their natural interactions with each other.

competition – in *ecology*, a relationship between two *organism*s for resources such as food, water, shelter or mates. Competition usually causes harm to both competing organisms.

conifer – member of a group of *tree*s that includes pines, firs, spruces, yews, cedars, and redwoods. Leaves are mostly evergreen and needle-shaped or scale-like. Most are *monoecious* with separate male and female cones.

conservation – in *biology*, the wise use of earth's natural resources including plants, animals, water, soil, and minerals; may involve deliberate management and protection to prevent unsustainable use or destruction.

conservation easement – voluntary legal agreement between a landowner and a government entity or land trust that limits uses of the land to protect its *conservation* values. Most are permanent but some may be for a designated period of time. Landowners are able to retain certain rights but give up others in order to provide public benefits such as water quality, *fish* and *wildlife habitat*, scenic views, and protection of rare *species*. Donation of a conservation easement can result in significant tax benefits for a landowner.

consumer – in *ecology*, an *organism* that eats plants or other animals. Four types of consumers include *carnivores, detritivores, herbivores,* and *omnivores*.

crepuscular – in animals, those active at twilight. Barn owls, cottontails, and bobcats are crepuscular. See *diurnal* and *nocturnal*.

crustacean – member of a large group of mainly *aquatic arthropods* that includes shrimp, crabs, lobsters, crawfish, barnacles, and krill.

cryptobiosis – temporary state in an *organism* during which life is absent or not detectable. Cryptobiotic crusts composed of *algae, fungi, moss*es, *lichen*s, and *bacteria* are found on the surface of some desert *habitat*s.

cultivar – plant variety that has been produced artificially by selective breeding of a wild plant. The many varieties of cultivated roses are cultivars of wild roses.

cursorial – adapted for running. Horses, wolves, and ostriches are cursorial animals.

NATURAL WORDS

D

deciduous – in woody plants, those that shed their leaves annually and remain leafless for an extended period of time.
decomposer – *organism* that breaks down lifeless *organic* materials and returns the resulting nutrients and minerals to the *ecosystem*. Most *bacteria* and *fungi* are decomposers.
dendrology – study of *tree*s, *shrub*s, and woody *vine*s.
dendrophile – person who loves trees.
dentition – arrangement, number and type (incisors, canines, premolars, molars) of teeth in an animal. *Mammal*s can often be identified to *species* by observing their teeth.
desert – area with an arid *environment*, often defined as having less than 10 inches of annual precipitation, and sparse vegetation.
detritivore – *organism* that feeds on *detritus*. Earthworms and dung beetles are detritivores.
detritus – in *ecology*, small particles of dead *organic* matter; may be parts of plants, animals, or their waste materials.

NATURAL WORDS

dicotyledon – largest of the two major groups of flowering plants; characterized by having two seed leaves (cotyledons) on embryonic plants; also called dicot. See *monocotyledon*.

dioecious – in plants, having male and female reproductive organs (flowers) on separate plants of the same *species*; an *adaptation* to avoid self-pollination. Maples, hollies, sumacs, and persimmons are examples of dioecious plants. See *monecious*.

diurnal – in animals, those active during the day. Monarch butterflies, fox squirrels, and red-tailed hawks are diurnal. See *nocturnal* and *crepuscular*.

dorsal – in animals, refers to the back.

drupe – in plants, fruits with seeds covered by a hard, stony tissue. Peaches, olives, and almonds are drupes.

NATURAL WORDS

E

echolocation – sonar-like navigation technique used by some animals like whales and bats. The animals produce sound waves that reflect off nearby surfaces and return to the sensory receptors (such as ears) of the animal.

ecology – study of the relationships between living *organism*s and their *environment*.

ecosystem – natural unit that includes the *organism*s within interacting with each other and with their non-living *environment* to complete their *life cycle*s using nutrients found mainly in that system (a closed cycle).

ecotone – transition area between two adjacent ecological *communities*; often contains plant and animal components of each community; scale can be large or small. As examples, an ecotone can be the interface between northern evergreen *forest*s and *tundra*, or the edge dividing a back yard and wood lot. See *edge effect*.

NATURAL WORDS

ectotherm – cold-blooded animal; one whose body temperature is regulated with external sources such as sunlight. *Reptile*s and *amphibian*s are ectotherms. See *endotherm*.

edge effect – tendency of some animals to prefer to use areas where two vegetative or land use types join, i.e., the edge. See *ecotone*.

effluent – liquid waste or sewage flowing into a water body; causes *environmenta*l damage in some cases.

endangered species – *organism* that is in danger of *extinct*ion in all or most of its range.

endemic – in *organism*s, those found only in a particular place. As examples, pronghorns are endemic to western North America, and some blind *fish* are endemic to specific caves.

endotherm – warm-blooded animal; an animal capable of producing and maintaining internal body heat. *Bird*s and *mammal*s are endotherms. See *ectotherm*.

energy – capacity to do work. Sources of energy include fossil fuels, geothermal, nuclear, and renewables such as solar, wind, and wave action.

environment – living and non-living surroundings of an *organism*.

eolian – pertaining to the wind, such as *soil*s formed, deposited or eroded by wind, including sediments and dunes.

epiphyte – plant attached to another plant for support; not parasitic on the support plant. Some orchids, *moss*es and *lichen*s are epiphytes on *tree*s.

estivation – state of dormancy in some animals that occurs during periods of hot, dry weather; a survival *adaptation*; similar to *hibernation* that occurs in cold weather. Some *amphibian*s and *reptile*s such as desert tortoises estivate.

estuary – typically *brackish water environment* where freshwater rivers meet the sea; a rich, productive *ecosystem* of plants and animals between fresh and saltwater. Chesapeake Bay is an estuary.

ethology – study of animal behavior.

eutrophication – process that occurs in water bodies with an influx of nutrients such as those in fertilizer, sewage, or *effluent*; may cause extreme *algae* growth that leads to oxygen depletion when the algae dies and is broken down by *bacteria*, resulting in die-offs of *fish* and other *organisms*.

evolution – changes that occur in all *organisms*, usually over long periods of time, that are a result of gene mutations and that enhance the organism's ability to survive and reproduce.

exoskeleton – rigid outer covering of some *invertebrates* such as in some *insects* and *crustaceans*.

exotic species – *species* not *native* to a specific area. White clover and house sparrows are exotic species in America. See *indigenous species* and *native species*.

extinct – condition of a *species* or group of *organisms* when living members no longer exist on earth. Passenger pigeons and saber-toothed tigers are extinct. See *extirpated*.

extirpated – condition when a *species* or group of *organisms* no longer exist in a specific geographic area, although they are still found elsewhere. Red wolves and American bison are extirpated in most of their historical range. See *extinct*.

extremophile – *organisms* that live in extreme *environments* hostile to most life on earth. Mostly microorganisms, their *habitats* include near-boiling water of deep-sea, hydrothermal vents, and acid-laden rocks within volcanos.

NATURAL WORDS

F

family – in *taxonomy*, one of the general divisions in the classification of *organism*s; between *order* and *genu*s. Asteraceae (sunflowers) and Bufonidae (toads) are examples of taxonomic families.

fauna – all the types of animals in a specified region, *habitat*, and/or time period. See *flora*.

fen – type of permanently saturated *wetland* receiving most of its water and nutrients from a ground source of water. Peat is often a component of fens.

feral – refers to domesticated animals that are surviving in the wild. Most domesticated animals can become feral in the appropriate *habitat*. Many cause serious harm to *native* plant and *wildlife population*s (e.g. feral cats and pigs).

fern – member of a group of flowerless plants that have leaf-like fronds and reproduce via *spore*s instead of seeds. More than 10,000 species are found around the world in *temperate* and *tropical* regions.

Fibonacci number – integers of a mathematical sequence that begin with 0 and 1, and each subsequent number is the

NATURAL WORDS

sum of the previous two (e.g. 0, 1, 1, 2, 3, 5, 8, 13...). The sequence is common in biological settings such as *tree* branching, *fern* frond spirals, pine cone bracts, design of spider webs and sea shells.

fish – cold-blooded *vertebrate* that breathes with gills and is restricted to an *aquatic habitat*. Most *species* have fins and scales.

floodplain – flat area of land adjacent to the banks of a stream or river that floods naturally if not impeded by levees or stream alterations; often has fertile soils and rich *biodiversity*.

flora – all the types of plants in a specified region, habitat, and/or time period. See *fauna*.

flyway – general routes of travel used by migratory *birds* during spring and fall *migration*. Four broad flyways are recognized in North America: Atlantic, Mississippi, Central, and Pacific.

food chain – chain of *organisms* in a *community* through which energy is transferred. Each animal link in the chain obtains energy by feeding on the link below it, and in turn passes the energy on when it is eaten by the next link. A chain typically begins with a green plant (a *producer*), which obtains energy via sunlight, and proceeds through *herbivores* and then *carnivores* (*consumers*).

food web – all of the *food chains* in a *community*.

forb – herbaceous plant that is not a grass, sedge or rush. Clovers and milkweeds are examples of forbs.

forest – *habitat* type in which *trees* are dominant, usually forming a closed *canopy*.

fossil fuel – fuel such as coal, oil, and natural gas that formed in the distant geological past by the decomposition of plants and animals. Extensive burning of fossil fuels as a source of energy increases carbon dioxide in the atmosphere and contributes to *global warming*.

NATURAL WORDS

fossorial – in animals, pertains to burrowing. Moles are fossorial *mammal*s.

frass – fine, powdery refuse and excrement produced by boring insects; also coarser excrement of caterpillars.

fry – small, recently hatched *fish*.

fungi – large group of *organism*s separated from other plants because they lack food-producing *chlorophyll*; include yeasts, rusts, smuts, mildews, molds, and mushrooms. Fungi obtain their food from other plants or decayed matter and are important *decomposer*s in *ecosystem*s.

G

gall – abnormal tumor-like growths that can occur on any part of a plant; caused mostly by *insect*s but also by mites, *fungi*, *bacteria*, and *virus*es.

game animal – wild animal that is managed and subject to legally regulated hunting. See *nongame*.

genus – in *taxonomy*, one of the general divisions in the classification of *organism*s; between *family* and *species*. *Homo* (humans) and *Pinus* (pines) are examples of genera. In writing, a genus is italicized.

gestation period – period of time from conception to birth in animals that bring forth live young (as opposed to egg layers). The gestation period of raccoons is about 63 days.

glabrous – in *botany*, plant parts having a smooth surface lacking hairs or down, especially leaves. See *pubescent* and *hirsute*.

glaciation – the process in which land is covered by glaciers and the impacts of the process.

global warming – a type of *climate change* where an increase in earth's temperature lasts for a decade or more. Current

NATURAL WORDS

global warming is caused by an increase in atmospheric carbon dioxide, believed by a wide majority of scientists to be the result of humans burning *fossil fuel*s. See also *climate*, *climate change*, and *weather*.

grassland – plant *community* where grasses are the dominant vegetation.

gravid – in animals, carrying eggs or young; pregnant.

grazer – in land *herbivore*s, those that eats mostly grasses (e.g. sheep and cattle); in *marine* communities, those *organism*s that feed on *algae* (e.g. certain *fish* and *crustacean*s). See *browser*.

greenhouse gas – any gas that when present in earth's atmosphere captures infrared radiation emitted from the earth's surface and redirects it back to the surface, potentially resulting in increased surface temperatures. Water vapor, carbon dioxide, and methane are greenhouse gases.

NATURAL WORDS

H

habitat – place where an *organism* lives; includes food, water, shelter, and space necessary for the organism to complete its *life cycle*.

habitat fragmentation – the breaking up of a large area of a particular *habitat* type into smaller units surrounded by a different habitat type. Residential or commercial development of a *prairie* or forested tract are examples.

halocline – in sea water, a well-defined, often abrupt change in the degree of *salinity* as one descends in the water column.

halophyte – in *botany*, plants that can tolerate very salty soil. Mangroves, switchgrass, and smooth cordgrass are examples of halophytes.

hammock – stand of *tree*s often appearing as an island in an otherwise open *ecosystem*; site is often slightly higher in elevation than surroundings. The term is most often used in the southeastern U.S. in places such as the Everglades.

hardwood forest – *forest* type dominated by *deciduous*, hardwood *tree species*.

NATURAL WORDS

heartwood – in *tree* trunks, the inner darker layers of wood often filled with disease-fighting natural chemicals that provide strength by resisting harmful *bacteria* and fungi. See *sapwood*.

herb – in *botany*, any small flowering plant or *fern* with a soft (not woody) stem.

herbarium – collection of dried plant specimens. Herbariums are critically important for several kinds of scientific research.

herbivore – *organism* that eats plants. See *carnivore*.

herpetology – study of *reptile*s and *amphibian*s.

hibernaculum – place where an *organism* seeks shelter for the winter, often to hibernate. Caves often serve as hibernacula for bats and bears; some *reptile*s and *insect*s burrow into leaf litter.

hibernation – state of winter dormancy occurring in some *mammal*s, *reptile*s and *amphibian*s during which time metabolism slows and body temperatures drop. See *estivation*.

hirsute – in *botany*, a plant part covered with stiff, coarse hairs. See *glabrous* and *pubescent*.

home range – area where an animal travels and lives throughout its *life cycle*.

host plant – food plant of a caterpillar. Pawpaws are host plants for zebra swallowtails.

humus – *organic* material derived from decaying animal and plant matter.

hybrid – offspring of two different *genera*, *species*, or varieties of *organism*s. A mule is a hybrid resulting from the cross of a male donkey and a female horse, which are different species.

hydric – in *ecology*, describes a wet *environment* or component thereof, such as soils.

hydrology – study of the earth's water, such as its distribution, circulation and movement.

NATURAL WORDS

I

ichthyology – study of *fish*.
imprinting – type of learning during which very young animals, especially *bird*s, realize their own species. Proper imprinting is crucial in order to learn survival skills such as correct foods to eat, predators to avoid, and mates to choose.
iNaturalist – multi-faceted *nature* app that helps *naturalist*s identify *organism*s world-wide, encourages interactions with other naturalists and scientists, and allows contributions of observations that can be used as research-quality data by anyone.
incubation period – in *ornithology*, the period of time beginning when the last egg of a clutch is laid until the eggs hatch. In most cases, incubation doesn't begin until all eggs are laid. The incubation period for robin eggs is usually 12 to 14 days.
indicator species – *organism* whose presence or absence serves as a measure of environmental conditions in a specific area. As examples, greasewood is an indicator

NATURAL WORDS

species for very alkaline soils in the western U.S., and the absence of *lichen*s in an area where they are normally found may indicate air *pollution* problems.

indigenous species – *species* that occurs naturally in a designated area; *native species*. See *exotic species*.

inorganic – in *biology*, describes a substance not made or derived from living matter. Rocks, minerals and metals are inorganic substances. See *organic*.

insect – type of *arthropod* that typically has three pairs of legs, one pair of antennae, and three distinct body parts (head, thorax, abdomen); most have wings. Insects include ants, bees, beetles, butterflies, fleas, lice, true bugs, greenflies, flies, termites, earwigs, cockroaches, silverfish, and springtails.

insectivore – animal or plant that feeds on *insect*s. Many *species* of *bird*s and bats and some types of plants such as Venus flytraps are insectivorous.

instar – in *arthropod*s such as *insect*s, a developmental stage between two *molt*s.

instinct – innate pattern of behavior in animals when exposed to certain stimuli. As examples, some young *mammals* have a natural instinct to swim when exposed to water, and all animals have an instinct to breed.

intertidal zone – the strip of seashore that is exposed at low tide and under water at high tide; also known as the littoral zone.

invasive species – *organism* that is not *native* to an *ecosystem* but that when present can harm the *environment*, economy, or human health. Fire ants, cane toads, and nutria are examples of invasive species in the U.S.

invertebrate – term for animals without backbones. Examples include *insect*s, worms, and snails.

iridescence – the display of lustrous, rainbow-like colors caused by light waves striking an *organism* with tissues having particular pigmentation and physical structure. Some

NATURAL WORDS

feathers, butterfly wings, beetle shells, and flower parts are iridescent.

NATURAL WORDS

K

keystone species – *organism* whose presence has a disproportionate impact on maintaining the *biodiversity* and general well-being of an *ecosystem*. Examples include grey wolves, elephants, and alligators.

kingdom – highest division of classification of *organism*s in Linnean *taxonomy*. The six kingdoms of life include Archaebacteria, Eubacteria, Protista, Fungi, Plantae (plants), and Animalia (animals).

L

lacustrine – pertaining to lakes, as in lacustrine *ecosystem*s or lacustrine deposits.

larva – stage of life in some animals between egg and adult; often very different in appearance from adult, such as tadpoles and caterpillars.

lateral line – sense organs in *fish* and some *aquatic amphibian*s consisting of pores arranged in a line down each side of the body; detects pressure changes and sound.

legume – plants that are in *family* Leguminosae consisting of beans, peas, and their relatives; also refers to the fruits (pods) of those plants.

lek – small area where animals such as prairie chickens and sage grouse gather to perform courtship rituals critical for mate selection and successful reproduction.

lentic – pertaining to or living in non-flowing water such as lakes and ponds. See *lotic*.

lenticel – small, raised pore on some plant stems that allow gas exchange between the plant and atmosphere.

lichen – compound *organism* consisting of an *algae* and *fungus*. In the *symbiotic* relationship the fungus often provides

NATURAL WORDS

supporting structure and the algae contributes food via *photosynthesis*.

life cycle – in *vertebrate*s, the entirety of the progressive series of changes in an animal beginning with fertilization and ending with death; in many plants and *invertebrate*s, there may be a succession of individuals involved when *asexual reproduction* occurs.

light pollution – excessive or obtrusive artificial light in the night sky; often causes serious ecological disruption and mortality in *organism*s such as migrating *bird*s and hatchling sea turtles.

limnology – study of freshwater *habitat*s and their inhabitants.

littoral zone – in lakes and other *aquatic habitat*s, the area that extends from the shoreline to a depth where sunlight no longer reaches the bottom; often the area where rooted aquatic plants can grow.

loam – rich *soil* composed of sand, clay, and *organic* matter.

loess – fine-grained, light-colored, fertile *soil* deposited by wind. See *alluvial soil*.

lotic – pertaining to or living in flowing water such as rivers and streams. See *lentic*.

M

mammal – *class* of warm-blooded, four-limbed *vertebrate*s with common characteristics that usually include hair, milk secretion, a diaphragm, and three bones in each middle ear. Most give birth to live young (and are not egg-layers). Humans, whales, bats, shrews, and armadillos are examples of mammals.

mammalogy – study of *mammal*s.

mariculture – cultivation of *marine* plants and animals in their natural *environment*.

marine – pertaining to or found in the sea.

marsh – *wetland* that is frequently or constantly flooded and dominated by herbaceous plants adapted to such conditions; often rich in nutrients and supporting abundant plant and animal life. Marshes may be fresh water, *brackish*, or salt water.

megafauna – large *mammal*s of a particular area or period of time.

melanism – in animals, an abnormally large amount of black pigment in the hair, feathers, or skin.

NATURAL WORDS

mesic – in *ecology*, a type of *environment* with a moderate supply of moisture; can also be used to describe plants that require moderate moisture. See *xeric*.

metamorphosis – in animals, the change from larval to adult stage; common in *insect*s (caterpillar to butterfly) and *amphibian*s (tadpole to frog). In insects, two types include complete metamorphosis with four life stages: egg, *larva*, *pupa*, and adult. Pupas do not resemble adults as in monarch butterflies; and incomplete metamorphosis with three stages: egg, nymph, and adult. Nymphs resemble small versions of adults as in lubber grasshoppers.

microclimate – the *climate* of small, specific sites in contrast to the general climate of the area. Microclimates can be found in caves and hot springs.

migration – seasonal movement of animals from one region to another, often to take advantage of more favorable food supplies, breeding *habitat*, or climatic conditions. Many diverse *species* migrate, e.g. American eels, monarch butterflies, humpback whales, elk, and ruby-throated hummingbirds.

mimicry – in *biology*, similarity in appearance of one *species* to another, often for protection from *predator*s; common in *insect*s when one or both species are poisonous or distasteful.

mitigation – an act that reduces the severity or harmful impacts of another action. *Environmenta*l mitigation sometimes occurs when projects that harm the environment require actions to offset the damages. Examples include the establishment of protected *conservation* areas or *afforestation* projects.

mobbing – in animals, a type of behavior in which one or more members of a *prey species* harass or attack a potential *predator*; most common in *bird*s with vulnerable eggs or young. As examples, wrens mob rat snakes and crows mob hawks.

NATURAL WORDS

mollusk – member of a group of *invertebrate*s that includes oysters, mussels, snails, octopuses, and their relatives. Mostly *aquatic*, some have hard shells.

molt – in animals, the normal, routine shedding of skin, shell, or feathers and the development of new ones, e.g. snakes shed skin, lobsters shed shell, *bird*s shed feathers.

monocotyledon – smaller of the two major groups of flowering plants; characterized by having one seed leaf (cotyledon) on embryonic plants; also called monocot. See *dicotyledon*.

monoculture – growing a crop consisting of one *species* only, generally even-aged. Millions of acres in the southern U.S. are a monoculture of loblolly pines.

monoecious – in plants, having separate male and female reproductive organs (flowers) on the same plant. Examples include oaks, pines, corn, and cucumbers. See *dioecious*.

moss – small, leafy-stemmed green plant that reproduces via *spore*s instead of flowers. Usually found in damp *habitat*s, mosses include many *species* such as sphagnum mosses.

murmuration – aerial maneuvers of a flock of starlings including swirling, pulsing, shrinking, and swelling masses of *bird*s; thought to be an aerial *predator* avoidance mechanism.

mutualism – relationship between two *organism*s in which both benefit from the interaction. Humans and their digestive gut *bacteria* have a mutualistic relationship, as do some bees and plants in the process of *pollination*. See *symbiosis*.

mycelium – in a *fungus*, the vegetative part consisting of many thread-like hyphae.

mycorrhiza – *symbiotic* or *parasitic* association of a *fungus* with the roots of a plant. Most plants have mycorrhiza. The fungus often helps the plant in the absorption of minerals and water, while the plant provides carbohydrate food to the fungus.

NATURAL WORDS

N

native species – *species* found naturally in a specified area; *indigenous species*. Mule deer are native to the western U.S. and sequoia trees are native in California. See *exotic species*.

natural history – study of living *organism*s and their non-living *environment*, usually by means of observations rather than formal experiments.

naturalist – student of *natural history*, as a hobby or professionally.

naturalization – in *biology*, process in which a *species* of *exotic organism* becomes established to the degree that a *population* is reproductively sustainable. Burmese pythons have become naturalized in the Everglades and Chinese tallow trees are naturalized in the southern U.S.

nature – physical world including all the plants, animals, and other *organism*s; includes geologic features such as *soil*, rocks, mountains, rivers, streams, and other non-living components; includes phenomena that occur on earth such as *weather*, earthquakes, *evolution*, reproduction, growth, and *decomposition*; usually includes only those components that originated independent of humans.

NATURAL WORDS

nectar – liquid comprised of sugars and other *organic* compounds, and produced by some plants, usually in the flowers, to encourage *pollination* by *insect*s and other animals.

niche – place or function of an *organism* or *population* of organisms in an ecological *community*.

nocturnal – active at night. Fireflies and owls are nocturnal. See *diurnal* and *crepuscular*.

nongame – *wildlife species* that are not legally hunted or trapped for food or sport. Songbirds, raptors and all endangered species are considered nongame. See *game animal*.

nonpoint source pollution – *pollution* that does not originate at a single source; often caused by rainfall moving across or through the ground and picking up pollutants in the process. See *pollution* and *point source pollution*.

nut – dry, single-seeded fruit with a hard, woody wall. Oaks and hickories produce nuts.

NATURAL WORDS

O

old growth forest – *forest* that has developed naturally over a long period of time without experiencing severe disturbance such as logging, windstorm, or fire that would set back *succession*. Characteristics vary but generally include presence of some *tree*s at least 120 years old, trees of different ages, large, dead snags, and large *vine*s in some *ecosystem*s.

omnivore – *organism* that eats both animal and plant materials. Raccoons and brown bears are omnivores. See *carnivore* and *herbivore*.

order – in *taxonomy*, one of the general divisions in the classification of *organism*s; between *class* and *family*. Coleoptera (beetles) and Squamata (lizards and snakes) are examples of taxonomic orders.

organic - in *biology*, describes a substance consisting of carbon compounds; often a product of life processes of plants and animals. Hair and leaf litter are examples of organic substances. See *inorganic*.

organism – something that is or was alive and carries out life processes such as growth, reproduction, and reaction to stimuli. All plants, animals, *bacteria*, *virus*es, *protist*s, and *fungi* are considered organisms.

ornithology – study of *bird*s.

overstory – in *ecology*, *tree*s that form the top layer of vegetation in a *forest* and shade all those beneath, including midstory, *shrubs*, and herbaceous *species* on the ground.

oviparous – to lay eggs with embryos that are still incompletely developed. *Bird*s, some *reptile*s and *fish*es are oviparous. See *viviparous* and *ovoviviparous*.

ovoviviparous – having eggs with embryos that develop and hatch inside the female *organism*. Some *insect*s, *fish*, lizards and snakes are ovoviviparous. See *oviparous* and *viviparous*.

NATURAL WORDS

P

parasite – *organism* that lives in or on another organism (the host), from which it gets nourishment. The host is often harmed in the relationship. Mistletoe, ticks and tapeworms are examples of parasites. See *symbiosis*.

passerine – in *ornithology*, a large group of *bird*s with feet adapted for perching. All songbirds and more than half of all *bird species* are passerines.

pathogen – *bacteria*, *virus*, *fungi*, or *parasite* that causes disease in another *organism*.

pelage – hair or fur on a *mammal*.

percolation – in the *water cycle*, the process of water flowing through the *soil*.

perennial – in plants, those herbaceous *species* that live for several years. Many *native* wildflowers and grasses are perennial. See *annual* and *biennial*.

permafrost – layer of permanently frozen *soil* below the surface of the ground in the frigid regions of the earth. *Climate change* is contributing to the recent loss of permafrost in some areas.

pesticide – chemical used to control or eradicate plants or animals.

NATURAL WORDS

petiole – stalk of a leaf that joins it to the stem.

phenology – study of periodic biological phenomena that are correlated with climatic or seasonal conditions. The timing of *bird migration* and flower bloom are examples of phenology topics.

phloem – living plant tissues that conduct sugars formed by *photosynthesis* (food) from leaves to other parts of the plant. See also *xylem*.

phoresy – non-parasitic association between two *organism*s when one travels on the body of another. As an example, flightless flower mites hitchhike on bees to travel from one flower to another.

photoperiod – in *biology*, the amount of time in a 24 hour period an *organism* is exposed to light. Photoperiodism affects the life processes of many organisms including plant growth and *bird migration*.

photosynthesis – process in which green plants, some *bacteria* and other *organism*s use energy from sunlight, water, and carbon dioxide to produce sugar as food with oxygen as a byproduct. Photosynthesis produces and maintains oxygen in the earth's atmosphere and provides a vital source of energy for most of the planet's organisms.

phototropism – growth or movement of an *organism* toward or away from light; most common in plants that grow toward sunlight.

phylum – in *taxonomy*, one of the general divisions of classification of *organisms*; between *kingdom* and *class*. Humans are in phylum Chordata.

phyllotaxy – in *botany*, the arrangement of leaves on a stem. Four types include alternate (one leaf per node that alternates on each side of the stem), spiral (one leaf per node with leaves that spiral around stem), opposite (two leaves per node and opposite each other), and whorled (three or more leaves per node). Leaf arrangement is often important in plant identification.

NATURAL WORDS

phytoplankton - type of *plankton* comprised of plants. See *plankton* and *zooplankton*.

pioneer species – animal or plant that moves into barren or disturbed areas to start a new cycle of life. In time they are often replaced with different *species*. Willows are pioneer species on newly formed sandbars.

plankton – microscopic plants (*phytoplankton*) and animals (*zooplankton*) that live in *aquatic habitat*s and function at the base of *food chain*s; ecologically critical either directly or indirectly as food source for *fish*, whales, and many other *species*.

plastron – part of a turtle's shell that covers the underside of the body. See *carapace*.

playa – shallow, circular depression that collects water and forms seasonal *wetland*s in areas such as the southwestern U.S. high plains; often critical *habitat* for *species* like migrating *waterfowl* and *shorebird*s.

poaching – violating hunting or fishing regulations such as seasons, limits, closed areas, size and sex restrictions.

pocosin – type of *wetland* found on the Atlantic coastal plain comprised of deep, saturated, peat *soil*s; often covered with *shrub*s or *tree*s; provides *habitat* for some rare plants.

point source pollution – *pollution* that originates at a specific, identifiable source, such as a fluid discharge pipe at a sewage treatment plant or a factory smokestack. See *nonpoint source pollution*.

pollen – fine, powdery particles produced in flowers and cones that contain male reproductive cells. See *pollination* and *pollinator*.

pollination – transfer of *pollen* from the male reproductive organs of a plant to the female reproductive organs, which enables the production of seeds. The transfer may be assisted by animals, wind, or water. See also *pollen* and *pollinator*.

NATURAL WORDS

pollinator – animal that transfers *pollen* to the female reproductive organs of a plant. Some bees, butterflies, bats, and hummingbirds are examples of pollinators. See *pollen* and *pollination*.

pollution – contamination of the earth (water, soil, or atmosphere) by the discharge of harmful substances.

population – in *ecology*, the members of one *species* of *organism* that live in a defined area, e.g. the deer population of Louisiana.

prairie – natural *habitat* type dominated by grasses; historically varied in size from small isolated tracts to millions of acres; often maintained by *soil* type, annual precipitation, or periodic fires. Prairies are often divided into shortgrass prairies and tallgrass prairies depending on the types of grasses present.

precocial – born or hatched in a well-developed state; soon capable of following their parents and feeding on their own. The young of jack rabbits and *waterfowl* are precocial.

predator – animal that kills and eats other animals. See also *prey*.

prescribed fire – planned and intentionally set fire in order to meet certain management objectives in a controlled setting. Prescribed fires are often used to maintain fire dependent *ecosystem*s such as *prairie*s and longleaf pine *forest*s.

prey – animals that are killed and eaten by other animals. See also *predator*.

primaries – longest flight feathers on a *bird*'s wing

producer – *organism* that manufactures its own food; types include green plants using

photosynthesis and some *bacteria* using chemical processes. Producers are eaten by *consumer*s.

protist – *organism*s in a group that cannot be classified as plants, animals, or *fungi*. Most are single-celled, but some like *algae* are not. Kelp is a protist.

NATURAL WORDS

protozoan – single-celled microscopic *organism*s enclosed in a cell membrane. Variable in shape and size, *Amoeba* and *Paramecium* are examples of protozoans.

psithurism – sound of rustling leaves such as that caused by wind in *tree*s.

pubescent - in *botany*, plant parts having a hairy surface. See *glabrous* and *hirsute*.

pupa – in *insect*s that exhibit complete *metamorphosis*, the developmental stage between *larva* and adult; also called chrysalis.

R

radial symmetry – in *biology*, body plan of some *organism*s that have parts arranged around a central axis. Some bottom-dwelling sea animals such as starfish and anemones have radial symmetry. See *bilateral symmetry*.

rain shadow – area on the leeward side of a mountain range that receives little precipitation because the mountains serve as a barrier to *weather* systems.

raptors – group of *predatory bird*s that includes eagles, hawks, and owls.

reforestation – planting *tree*s in a cleared area that was historically forested; also sometimes called afforestation, which more correctly defines planting trees on areas that were not historically *forest* lands. Thousands of acres in the Lower Mississippi River Valley that were cleared for agriculture have been reforested since 1980.

relict community – *community* of *organism*s that once had a much wider distribution but occurs now only very locally.

renewable resource – natural part of the *environment* that when used (consumed) has the capability to replenish or reproduce itself in the right conditions on a human time

NATURAL WORDS

scale. Solar energy, fresh water, and *forest*s are examples of potential renewable resources.

reptiles – group of *ectothermic*, *vertebrate* animals that includes snakes, lizards, crocodilians, turtles, and tortoises. Most *species* have dry, scaly skin and lay eggs (although not all).

respiration – in animals, the movement of air or dissolved gases into and out of the lungs, which results in physical and chemical processes that carry oxygen to cells and remove carbon dioxide and water.

rhizome – in plants, an underground stem with buds that can grow into shoots as a type of vegetative reproduction.

riparian – in *ecology*, refers to anything located on or pertaining to areas along streams, rivers, or lakes. Examples include riparian *wildlife*, riparian plants, riparian *habitat*, and riparian *ecosystem*s.

riverine – in *ecology*, related to or found along a river or riverbank; more specific than *riparian*.

rookery – term for a breeding colony of some types of animals, usually *bird*s. In North America, often used in reference to colonies of wading *bird*s such as egrets, herons, and ibises.

S

salinity – in *nature*, the relative proportion of salt in a body of water. Fresh water is defined as having 0 - .5 parts per thousand (ppt) of salt; *brackish* water .5 – 30 ppt; saline water (sea water) 30 – 50 ppt; and briny water 50+ ppt.

samara – in plants, a small dry seed with wing-like growths that aid in wind dispersal. Maples and ashes are examples of *tree*s that produce samaras.

saprophyte – *organism* that obtains all of its nutrients from dead *organic* matter. Some plants, *fungi*, and *bacteria* are saprophytes; all are *consumers*.

sapwood – in *tree* trunks, the outer layer of light colored wood that contains *xylem* vessels. See *heartwood*.

savanna – flat region of grassland with scattered *tree*s found in *tropical* and subtropical *ecosystem*s.

scat – fecal droppings of an animal.

scavenger – animal that feeds on dead, decaying *organism*s. Vultures are obligate scavengers, meaning that is all they eat. Other animals such as coyotes are facultative scavengers, meaning they get some of their food in other ways such as *predation*. *Invertebrate*s such as blowflies and yellowjackets can also be scavengers.

NATURAL WORDS

scientific method – type of research that involves identifying a problem, gathering relevant data, forming a hypothesis based on the data, and testing the hypothesis by experiment. The scientific method is used to advance knowledge of science.

scute – large scale or plate such as those that cover a turtle's shell or an alligator's back.

sea level – level of the earth's oceans as a reference point to measure elevations of geographic features such as hilltops.

seed – in plants, the fertilized structure containing an embryo that develops into a new plant. Seeds develop in fruits or cones depending on the type of plant.

sere – in *ecology*, the series of plant *succession* stages in an area that leads to a *climax community*, e.g. from bare ground to a climax *forest*.

sexual reproduction – creation of a new *organism* by combining genes in the reproductive cells of two parent organisms; the most common type of reproduction in plants and animals. See *asexual reproduction*.

shorebirds – in *ornithology*, a group of *bird*s that frequents shallow water, mud flats, and shorelines along rivers, lakes, oceans, and other water bodies. Shorebirds include many species of sandpipers, plovers, and related families.

shrub – small, woody *perennial* plant usually less than 15 feet in height with many branches.

small game – small *species* of animals that are hunted for food and/or sport. Small game animals are usually *mammal*s like rabbits and squirrels, or *bird*s such as quail and ducks. See *big game*.

smolt – stage of a young salmon's life when it turns silvery and migrates from freshwater to the sea for the first time.

soil – various mixtures of *inorganic* weathered rock and minerals in the form of sand, silt and clay plus an *organic* component of *humus*.

NATURAL WORDS

spawn – as a verb, the release of eggs and sperm into the water for reproduction by *fish* and some *aquatic amphibian*s; as a noun, the actual released eggs and sperm.

species – in *taxonomy*, one of the general divisions in the classification of *organism*s; usually the smallest major unit (although *subspecies* and varieties are sometimes listed) and one step below *genus*. Organisms of the same species are very similar and can successfully breed with each other; *sapiens* (human) and *lotor* (raccoon) are examples of species names. In writing, species is italicized but not capitalized.

spore – tiny reproductive cell capable of developing into a new *organism* without the involvement of *sexual reproduction*. Spores are part of the *life cycle*s of many plants, *fungi*, *algae*, and *protozoan*s. Some spores are very durable in the *environment* and remain viable for many years.

stamen – *pollen*-bearing organ of a flower

stomata – pores in the surface of leaves that can open or close to regulate evaporation of water from the leaf and entry of carbon dioxide into the leaf.

subsidence – in geology, the settling or sinking of the earth's surface as a result of geologic processes, manmade causes, or a combination of both. Louisiana is losing vast amounts of coastal *wetland*s as a result of subsidence caused by natural and human actions.

subspecies – in *taxonomy*, a subdivision of *species*. Subspecies within a species are very similar and often capable of breeding, although they usually don't because they live in different places.

succession – in *ecology*, the change in composition of plant *communities* over time, often beginning with colonization of a site and ending with climax vegetation. The stages of succession in a given area can be altered or set back by natural or manmade disturbances such as fire or logging. Animal communities often change along with plant succession, and some are dependent on a specific stage. For example, wood thrushes thrive in mature hardwood *forest*s. See *sere*.

swamp – *wetland* that is dominated by woody plants. A critical characteristic is the water table must recede often enough to a depth that allows root aeration and survival of adapted *tree*s and *shrub*s.

symbiosis – close relationship between two different *organism*s. The types of symbiosis include *commensalism* where one organism benefits and the other is neither harmed nor helped; *parasitism* where one organism benefits and the other is harmed; and *mutualism* where both organisms benefit.

NATURAL WORDS

T

tapetum lucidum – layer of the retina in eyes of some *vertebrate* animals and spiders that reflects light . The color of reflected light varies by *species*. Horses have blue eyeshine, *fish* have white eyeshine, and that of the opossum and many rodents is red. The eyeshine of cats and *canid*s is yellow.

taproot – principal large root that grows vertically in some plants.

taxonomy – study of the classification of *organism*s based on their similarities and differences.

temperate – *climate* free of extreme temperatures. Temperate climates generally exit between the *tropics* and polar regions worldwide.

temperature-dependent sex determination (TSD) – in some *reptile*s, a reproductive process during which the sex of young animals is determined by the temperature of eggs during *incubation*. In American alligators, constant incubation temperatures between 84° and 88°F will result in all females. Between 88° and 90°F, a mixture of sexes will develop. Incubation at 91-92° will produce all males. Other crocodilians and some turtles also exhibit TSD.

NATURAL WORDS

terrestrial – in *biology*, describes an *organism* that lives on land; also defines some ecological terms as land-based, such as terrestrial *habitat* or terrestrial *communities*. See *aquatic*, *arboreal*, and *fossorial*.

territory – in some animals, the part of their *habitat* that is defended from encroachment by others of the same *species*. Many kinds of *mammal*s, *bird*s, *fish*, and *reptile*s establish territories, usually as a part of breeding behavior or protection of food resources.

thermocline – layer of water in the oceans and some lakes that separates a much warmer body of water above from much cooler water below.

topography – arrangement, shape, and relative position of natural features such as swamps, hills, and rivers on a designated area of land.

topsoil – upper layer of soil often containing *organic* matter. Most plants get nutrients and minerals from topsoil.

transpiration – process in which plants transport water up from roots to evaporate through microscopic openings (*stomata*) on the bottom of leaves. Transpiration serves three critical roles in plants: the water movement provides an avenue of transport for minerals and food throughout the plant; it cools the plant (and incidentally humans, as 80 percent of the cooling effect of a shade tree is from the evaporative cooling of transpiration); and it maintains turgor pressure in cells, which allows plant parts to remain firm and upright. When the amount of moisture in the *soil* fails to keep up with the rate of transpiration, loss of turgor pressure occurs and the stomata close; transpiration plummets and the plant wilts.

tree – large, woody, *perennial* plant with a trunk and often limbs.

tributary – stream or river that flows into a larger river or water body. The Missouri River is a tributary of the Mississippi River.

NATURAL WORDS

trophic level – in *ecology*, the position of an *organism* in a *food chain* or *food web*. A plant always occupies the lowest trophic level, followed by an organism that eats the plant.

tropical – refers to regions of the earth with little temperature and length of daylight variation throughout the year; includes most areas near the equator.

tundra – type of *biome* comprising vast areas of arctic and subarctic regions in the northern hemisphere. Characteristics include permanently frozen subsoil, flat topography, lack of *tree*s, and dominant vegetation consisting of *moss*es, *lichen*s, *herb*s, and small *shrub*s.

U

umwelt – *environment* as it is perceived by an *organism*. The umwelt for any creature is dependent upon the types of sensory receptors it possesses and its capability to process stimuli of those receptors. Human awareness is based on the senses of sight, smell, touch, hearing and taste, each with its own limits. Some organisms have these senses and/or different ones that function within different parameters.

understory – part of a *forest* consisting of plants growing beneath the *canopy*; may include saplings, *shrub*s, and *herb*aceous *species*.

NATURAL WORDS

V

ventral – in animals, the under or lower surface; e.g. the belly of a lizard.

vernal – pertaining to the spring season.

vertebrate – animal that has a spinal cord surrounded and protected by cartilage or bone (i.e. a backbone). *Bird*s, *mammal*s, *fish*, *reptile*s, and *amphibian*s are vertebrates.

vine – broadly defined as any climbing plant. Vines have evolved different mechanisms to climb including twining their stems around a support, or using specialized roots, tendrils, or flowers to clasp a support in order to reach sunlight or nutrients.

virus – microscopic particle that can infect the cells of living *organism*s, the only place they can replicate. Viruses are sometimes considered nonliving as they do not meet the criteria in definitions of living organisms. They often cause diseases in human hosts such as the common cold, influenza, smallpox, measles, and yellow fever. Wild plants and animals are also vulnerable to many destructive viruses.

viviparous – type of reproductive process in some animals in which embryos develop inside the female often with the

NATURAL WORDS

aid of a placenta. Most *mammal*s, including humans, are viviparous. See *oviparous* and *ovoviviparous*.

NATURAL WORDS

W

water cycle – natural, continuous movement of water on earth that includes evaporation of water from the surface, its uplift into the atmosphere as vapor where it cools and condenses into precipitation to fall again to the surface; also called hydrologic cycle.

waterfowl – in *ornithology*, generally refers to members of the Anatidae *family* such as ducks, geese, and swans.

watershed – area of a landscape that drains into a specified water body such as a river or bay. Watersheds can be as small as the area that feeds into an ephemeral stream or as large as the territory that drains into the Mississippi River.

weather – short term atmospheric conditions such as temperature, relative humidity, precipitation, and storm activity. See *climate*, *climate change* and *global warming*.

wetland – area where the water table is at or near the surface for most of the growing season in most years, resulting in soil saturation and dominant plants that are adapted to wet conditions. The many types of wetlands can vary in size up to entire *ecosystem*s.

NATURAL WORDS

wildlife – animals that are not tame or domesticated and that are not naturally dependent on humans for their existence.

NATURAL WORDS

X

xeric – in *ecology*, a type of *environment* with little moisture; very dry; xerophytes are plants that require little moisture. See *mesic*.

xylem – in plants, the tube-like vessels that transport water and nutrients up from the roots to stems and leaves. Most xylem cells are not living. See *phloem*.

NATURAL WORDS

Z

zoology – study of animals.
zooplankton – type of *plankton* comprised of animals. See *plankton* and *phytoplankton*.

NATURAL WORDS

About the Authors

Amy Ouchley is a naturalist and environmental educator. She conducts encounters with the outdoors for students and teachers, children and adults, through workshops, field trips, and conferences, as well as programs in schools, libraries, nature centers and museums. Her book, *Swamper – Letters from a Louisiana Swamp Rabbit*, is widely used to teach environmental education in 4th through 7th grade classrooms. She has received the Louisiana Wildlife Federation's Conservation Educator of the Year Award.

Kelby Ouchley is a writer, public speaker, and retired biologist and manager of national wildlife refuges for the U.S. Fish & Wildlife Service. Since 1995 he has written and narrated *Bayou-Diversity*, an award-winning weekly conservation program on public radio. He is the author of *Flora and Fauna of the Civil War; Bayou-Diversity: Nature and People in the Louisiana Bayou Country; Bayou-Diversity 2; American Alligator: Ancient Predator in the Modern World;* and the novel *Iron Branch*. Kelby and his wife Amy live in Rocky Branch, Louisiana on the edge of the D'Arbonne Swamp.

Contact Information
Website: https://www.bayou-diversity.com/
Bayou-Diversity Facebook page:
https://www.facebook.com/BayouDiversity/?ref=bookmarks

Made in the USA
Columbia, SC
06 May 2025